T0026994

TRENDS IN SOUTHEAST ASIA

The **ISEAS – Yusof Ishak Institute** (formerly Institute of Southeast Asian Studies) is an autonomous organization established in 1968. It is a regional centre dedicated to the study of socio-political, security, and economic trends and developments in Southeast Asia and its wider geostrategic and economic environment. The Institute's research programmes are grouped under Regional Economic Studies (RES), Regional Strategic and Political Studies (RSPS), and Regional Social and Cultural Studies (RSCS). The Institute is also home to the ASEAN Studies Centre (ASC), the Singapore APEC Study Centre and the Temasek History Research Centre (THRC).

ISEAS Publishing, an established academic press, has issued more than 2,000 books and journals. It is the largest scholarly publisher of research about Southeast Asia from within the region. ISEAS Publishing works with many other academic and trade publishers and distributors to disseminate important research and analyses from and about Southeast Asia to the rest of the world.

SME RESPONSES TO CLIMATE CHANGE IN SOUTHEAST ASIA

Michael T. Schaper

ISSUE
2
2022

ISEAS YUSOF ISHAK
INSTITUTE

Published by: ISEAS Publishing
                  30 Heng Mui Keng Terrace
                  Singapore 119614
                  publish@iseas.edu.sg
                  http://bookshop.iseas.edu.sg

© 2022 ISEAS – Yusof Ishak Institute, Singapore

All rights reserved. No part of this publication may be reproduced, stored in a retrieval system, or transmitted in any form, or by any means, electronic, mechanical, photocopying, recording or otherwise, without prior permission.

The author is wholly responsible for the views expressed in this book which do not necessarily reflect those of the publisher.

ISEAS Library Cataloguing-in-Publication Data

Name(s): Schaper, Michael T., author.
Title: SME responses to climate change in Southeast Asia / by Michael T. Schaper.
Description: Singapore : ISEAS-Yusof Ishak Institute, January 2022. | Series: Trends in Southeast Asia, ISSN 0219-3213 ; TRS2/22 | Includes bibliographical references.
Identifiers: ISBN 9789815011296 (soft cover) | ISBN 9789815011302 (pdf)
Subjects: LCSH: Small business—Southeast Asia. | Climate change mitigation—Southeast Asia.
Classification: LCC DS501 I59T no. 2(2022)

Typeset by Superskill Graphics Pte Ltd
Printed in Singapore by Mainland Press Pte Ltd

FOREWORD

The economic, political, strategic and cultural dynamism in Southeast Asia has gained added relevance in recent years with the spectacular rise of giant economies in East and South Asia. This has drawn greater attention to the region and to the enhanced role it now plays in international relations and global economics.

The sustained effort made by Southeast Asian nations since 1967 towards a peaceful and gradual integration of their economies has had indubitable success, and perhaps as a consequence of this, most of these countries are undergoing deep political and social changes domestically and are constructing innovative solutions to meet new international challenges. Big Power tensions continue to be played out in the neighbourhood despite the tradition of neutrality exercised by the Association of Southeast Asian Nations (ASEAN).

The **Trends in Southeast Asia** series acts as a platform for serious analyses by selected authors who are experts in their fields. It is aimed at encouraging policymakers and scholars to contemplate the diversity and dynamism of this exciting region.

THE EDITORS

Series Chairman:
    Choi Shing Kwok

Series Editor:
    Ooi Kee Beng

Editorial Committee:
    Daljit Singh
    Francis E. Hutchinson
    Norshahril Saat

SME Responses to Climate Change in Southeast Asia

By Michael T. Schaper

EXECUTIVE SUMMARY

- Micro-, small- and medium-sized enterprises (SMEs) account for approximately 97 per cent of all active business entities within the ASEAN region. They are an important contributor to both emissions generation and future reduction.
- A recent large-scale, multi-country quantitative assessment was undertaken into how SMEs are dealing with climate change in Indonesia, Malaysia, the Philippines, Singapore and Vietnam. Most respondents reported a high level of concern about climate change.
- Over 90 per cent of firms are currently undertaking measures to reduce emissions, albeit that they are typically simple steps such as reducing air conditioning and electricity, recycling or installing low-energy lighting.
- Common intentions to deal with future extreme weather events include reducing emissions, developing a disaster plan, or reviewing business insurance policies.
- Major obstacles to dealing with climate issues are firstly, a lack of knowledge and secondly, insufficient funds. Governments are the preferred source of information, followed by business associations/chambers, friends and family. Social media, YouTube and websites are overwhelmingly the dissemination modes of choice. There were significant variations in these patterns from one reporting country to another.
- Policymakers can help SMEs adjust to climate change by: encouraging them to adopt simple emission reduction measures; providing training and financial support; ensuring appropriate online delivery of advisory and assistance measures; and localising responses to meet the needs of SMEs which are specific to different ASEAN member states.

SME Responses to Climate Change in Southeast Asia

By Michael T. Schaper[1]

INTRODUCTION

Climate change is not only one of the great challenges of this century for governments and individuals; it is also a major issue for the millions of micro-, small- and medium-sized businesses (SMEs) that exist across Southeast Asia.

The current level of knowledge about the impact of climate change on this sector is low. There are a number of important questions for which more evidence is needed: Do small business operators think climate change is an important issue? How are SMEs in the region attempting to reduce their emissions, if at all? What do they intend to do in future to deal with a warming climate? What obstacles do they face? And what effective assistance and advice are needed for them to deal with the issue?

This paper summarizes the results of a large-scale, multi-country quantitative assessment of these issues, focusing on SMEs in the five largest economies in ASEAN. The results are illuminating, and provide some guidelines for policymakers, governments, industry associations and climate change advocates as they grapple with the complex issue of helping SMEs work towards a low-emissions future economy.

CLIMATE CHANGE

As Table 1 indicates, every nation in ASEAN already contributes to some extent to the continuing global output of GHG-inducing emissions, such

---

[1] Michael T. Schaper is Visiting Senior Fellow at the ISEAS – Yusof Ishak Institute, Singapore and Adjunct Professor with the John Curtin Institute of Public Policy, Curtin University, Western Australia.

Table 1: Territorial CO₂ Emissions amongst ASEAN Nations in 2020

	MTCO$_2$	Population (approx.)
Brunei	10	0.44 million
Cambodia	15	16.7 million
Indonesia	590	273.5 million
Laos	34	7.3 million
Malaysia	273	32.4 million
Myanmar	36	54 million
The Philippines	136	109.5 million
Singapore	46	5.8 million
Thailand	258	69.8 million
Vietnam	254	97.3 million
Total	1,652	

Source: Global Carbon Project (2021). MTCO$_2$ = million metric tons of carbon dioxide. "Territorial" = emitted within the designated country. Global total in 2021 was 34,807 MTCO$_2$.

as CO$_2$. Whilst some member states (such as Brunei and Cambodia) produce very low levels, others such as Indonesia are already amongst the biggest generators of emissions globally.

Climate change is already having a tangible impact on the region, according to the Intergovernmental Panel on Climate Change (IPCC). A number of physical changes are already occurring in the climate and weather patterns of Southeast Asia. These include alterations to monsoon patterns; more heatwaves, cyclonic activity and droughts; rising sea levels; and more precipitation and flooding. The IPCC predicts that as temperatures continue to rise, these problems will be exacerbated, noting that "every additional 0.5°C of global warming causes clearly discernible increases in the intensity and frequency of hot extremes, including heatwaves, and heavy precipitation ... There will be an increasing occurrence of some extreme events unprecedented in the observational record with additional global warming..." (IPCC 2021, p. SPM-19).

Finally, sea level rises are also "virtually certain" and will threaten major metropolitan regions such as those in Manila, Bangkok and Jakarta (ASEAN 2021).

Some modelling suggests that ASEAN economies will be especially badly hit by global warming and will suffer some of the largest declines in GDP globally. Whilst the region might expect to suffer a 4 per cent GDP decrease if temperatures increase by 2°Celsius, this could potentially blow out to 37 per cent if temperatures rise above that point. Conversely, the region is also likely to gain the greatest upswing benefit if warming can be confined under the 2°Celsius Paris Agreement limits (Swiss Re Institute 2021, p. 1).

These concerns are also now echoed by many residents of the region. Recent examinations of community attitudes suggest that Southeast Asians think that more should be done to address climate change issues, with a majority viewing climate change to be as much of a crisis as the COVID-19 pandemic, whilst also expressing some reservations about ASEAN's effectiveness as a regional body to deal with the problem (Seah, Martinus and Qiu 2021).

Both globally and in the region, the evidence shows that business commercial activities and industrial outputs are a major contributor to GHG emissions. The sixth IPCC report suggests that industry accounts for approximately 24 per cent of GHG emissions (see Table 2). However, in practice, many such figures underestimate the overall contribution of business activity, placing many commercial emissions into other categories, such as land-use or transport, rather than designating them to be part of the "industry" sector. Specific figures on total business-related GHG emissions in the ASEAN are even more difficult to accurately obtain, as the region is often placed together with other zones (such as the broader Asia-Pacific, or with North Asia) when data is published. Nevertheless, although the intensity of emissions varies from one firm and one industry sector to another, all businesses are to some extent contributors to the problem.

Traditionally, most carbon-reduction efforts in the business sector have been focused on large-scale corporations, multinational companies and on firms in heavy industries, with the broader SME sector being often overlooked by policymakers, regulators and climate change

Table 2: Global Emissions (GtCO₂eq) by Major General Sector

Energy systems	20 GtCO$_2$eq	34%
Industry	14 GtCO$_2$eq	24%
Agriculture, forestry and other land uses	12 GtCO$_2$eq	21%
Transport	8.3 GtCO$_2$eq	14%
Buildings	3.3 GtCO$_2$eq	6%
Total	57.6	99%

Source: Lamb and Wiedmann (2021). GtCO$_2$eq: gigatonnes of equivalent carbon dioxide.

advocates. However, in the last decade this omission has begun to be rectified, as it has become increasingly accepted that even the smallest enterprise emits some carbon, and that collectively the SME sector's emissions footprint is significant (Blundel and Hampton 2021). Whilst there are few (if any) accurate estimates at the national or regional level of their contribution (Blundel and Hampton 2021), the United Nations' Framework Convention on Climate Change has now begun to argue that "private sector action, including that by SMEs, will be critical in addressing climate change" (UNFCCC/UNESCAP 2021, p. 1).

Assessments by the OECD and ERIA of the role of ASEAN governments in assisting SMEs to deal with these and other environmental issues have argued that "specific effort to support SMEs are relatively rare in the region … there is substantial room for progress". It noted that although most countries do provide some support to private enterprise, the policy frameworks, regulatory incentives and funding support offered were highly variable from one country to the next, and often tended to favour larger firms over SMEs. In many cases, responsibilities were split between different arms of government, with SME development agencies and environmental bodies often working separately from each other (OECD/ERIA 2018, p. 72). Singapore, Malaysia and Vietnam were noted as leading best practice in the region for many activities, whilst Cambodia, Myanmar, Brunei and Laos were regarded as "early stage" in their processes. Most countries had adopted some industry sector-specific programmes (such as those for the automotive industry in the Philippines, for manufacturing in Cambodia, and for the construction sector in Malaysia), but more needed to be done to create genuinely nationwide, whole-of-government approaches when dealing with SMEs. The authors also noted an informational gap, and recommended more work to develop effective communication strategies and advisory services to reach out to SMEs (OECD/ERIA 2020, p. 18).

SMEs IN ASEAN

Micro-, small- and medium-sized enterprises form the majority of businesses at both the global level and within the ASEAN region. With more than 70 million SMEs currently in existence across Southeast Asia, they account for approximately 97 per cent of all active firms, generate around 40 per cent of GDP, and employ almost 70 per cent of the workforce (ADB 2020). Table 3 shows a breakdown of small firm numbers on a country-by-country basis.

Interestingly, there is no common definition of what constitutes an SME within ASEAN. Unlike other regional bodies such as the European Union, each nation in Southeast Asian employs its own set of metrics to define and measure SMEs, using differing combinations of information relating to number of employees, annual sales turnover, assets and amount of capital invested (ABD 2020).[2]

Substantial evidence suggests that SMEs cannot be treated simply as a "shrunken down" version of a larger corporation when it comes to climate change management (Curran and Blackburn 2001). An SME is not simply a smaller version of a larger corporate enterprise; it is a fundamentally different type of business organization. This also gives rise to a number of substantial asymmetries in business resources, operation and management, all of which are relevant to the issue of how different sized-firms respond to climate change (see Table 4).

---

[2] These different criteria are also listed in the ADB report (2020, p. 12).

Table 3: Number of SMEs in Southeast Asia

	Number of SMEs	Total Number of Businesses	SMEs as % of All Firms	Persons Employed by SMEs
Brunei (2017)	5,900	6,000	97.2%	66,100
Cambodia (2019)	460,000	510,000	90% +	1,200,000
Indonesia (2018)	64,194,000	64,199,600	99.9%	116,978,600
Laos (2006)	114,200	126,900	90%	Not available
Malaysia (2016)	907,100	921,000	98.5%	Not available
Myanmar (2015)	114,200	126,900	Not available	Not available
The Philippines (2018)	995,745	1,000,506	99.5%	5,714,200
Singapore (2019)	271,800	273,100	99.5%	2,520,000
Thailand (2018)	3,077,800	3,084,300	99.8%	13,950,200
Vietnam (2019)	744,800	760,000	98%	Not available
Total	70,888,100	71,010,900	99.8%	140,429,100

Note: Figures rounded to the nearest hundred. Myanmar SME count not provided, so figures are imputed as conservatively being 90 per cent of all firms.
Source: Schaper (2020).

Table 4: Differences between SMEs and Large Firms Dealing with Climate Change

	SMEs	Large Firms
Number of business establishments	Single	Multiple
Exposure to different geographic regions	Low	High
Level of emissions	Low	High
Ability to measure GHGs	Low	High
Compliance cost burden	Proportionately high	Proportionately low
Knowledge of, and to access to, relevant information	Limited; ad hoc	Sophisticated; extensive
Access to technical experts and training capabilities	Limited	High
Financial capacity to fund climate initiatives	Typically small and limited	Substantial
Use of external carbon advisers	Limited; ad hoc	Systematic; structured

Despite the large numbers of SMEs in existence and their economic and environmental significance, there is a surprising shortage of research into the issue of climate change and SMEs. Even the IPCC reports (2014, 2021) do not discuss or analyse the phenomenon in any detail when examining industrial emissions. Traditionally, the focus of much climate change abatement and adjustment by business has been centred on large firms. This is because such enterprises are limited in number (and thus easy to identify and engage with), usually generate a much larger and easily identified carbon footprint, have considerable capacity to undertake abatement activities, and can generate highly visible and easily-measurable results that are often publicly reported (such as through stock market disclosure requirements) (Amran et al. 2016). Even when SMEs are identified as a priority area, the focus is often on the limited group of medium-sized firms (often known in Europe as the *mittelstand*), rather than the smaller-scale enterprises that make up the vast majority of the SME sector (Storbeck 2018).

This is beginning to change, however, but even research journals dedicated to the issues of business and the environment, sustainability, and associated matters appear to have published only a limited range of papers on the SME-climate change nexus to date.[3] As one commentator has noted: "The existing literature and knowledge … is a relatively underdeveloped field, empirical evidence for it being sparse … surprisingly little is known about these issues in practice" (Schaer and Kuruppu 2018, pp. 7, 9).

A first matter to understand is the personal level of concern about climate change amongst SME owners and managers. This is important. Since most small firms are directly managed and operated by their owners; personal values can impact on management decisions.

Whilst there has been little direct examination of this issue in Southeast Asian firms, evidence from other nations (such as the United Kingdom, Australia, the European Union, Canada and the United States) indicates that there is actually a substantial number of SME operators who seek to reduce emissions. A principal driver is often a sense of altruism or their own personal environmental or sustainability values; in some cases, though, it may also be a strategic decision to proactively adapt to climate change and so reduce potential losses and damage.

The exact size of this group is hard to determine, but they tend to be the firms who will choose to adopt best practice greening and climate-friendly activities as a personal commitment, regardless of the costs or benefits from doing so (Schaer and Kuruppu 2018; Williams and

---

[3] For example, a search of the well-established, long-running refereed journal *Business Strategy and the Environment* yielded only a handful of articles on the search terms "climate change AND SMEs" for the period up until mid-2021. Likewise, Linnenluecke and Smith (2018) found only about two dozen articles on this issue within peer-reviewed scholarly journals.

Schaefer 2012; Schaper 2019; Schaefer, Williams and Blundel 2020). In fact, this group may be much bigger than expected: a 2019 survey of approximately 560 SMEs in the United Kingdom, for example, found that almost 90 per cent of respondents were aware of climate change as an issue requiring action, and supported this stance (Carbon Trust 2020).

However, many of these same respondents report being hamstrung by a lack of time, money (resources), and outside support and assistance from being able to implement the decarbonization changes they would like to adopt.

The second issue is that of reducing the quantum of emissions produced by SMEs.

There are numerous ways in which SMEs can be encouraged to reduce their emissions—so much so, in fact, that one recent review of these has concluded that today "there is a plethora of tools and approaches available to support SMEs to reduce carbon emissions" (Blundel and Hampton 2021, p. 3). These can include improvements in energy usage; more efficient usage of transport; improvements to in-house operating and manufacturing processes; measuring their own current GHG emissions; involvement in green certification programmes; purchasing of carbon credits; and a number of other tools.

These individual measures are not described in detail in this paper, but rather are shown in terms of increasing sophistication in Table 5. There is potentially a very wide menu of options that individual firms and managers can choose to act upon, and there is no "one size fits all" best course of action for all firms.

Indeed, Schaer and Kuruppu (2018) have argued that there can be substantial variation between industries as to what form emissions reduction should take (a hotel or a retail store, for example, is likely to focus on quite different emissions from what a small foundry or a farm would do), and so decisions are best made at the individual firm level.

The third issue is that of SME responses to extreme weather events (EWE).

Most surveys of SMEs in recent years have revealed a growing awareness that climate change is leading to more adverse natural events (Zurich Insurance 2016). In many cases, though, the same studies indicate that most firms are unprepared, and are more likely to belatedly

Table 5: Practical Internal Actions to Reduce Firm GHG Emissions

Simple, easy, low cost	Installing low-energy lighting
	Reducing air conditioning usage
	Turning off electrical devices when not in use
	Sourcing low-emission products/services (raw materials) for own use
	Recycling/reusing business waste
	Staff training
	Using/purchasing hybrid/electric vehicles
	Measuring energy usage (via smart meters or similar)
	Purchasing from, or installing inhouse, renewable energy sources
	Participating in green certification programmes, EMS systems (such as ISO 14000)
	Reducing work-related travel
	Working from home instead of an office
	Purchasing GHG offsets
	Reconfiguring transport to reduce carbon miles
Complex, resource (time/money/effort) intensive	Green financing tools
	Reconfiguring packaging to reduce volume, carbon miles
	Building retrofits/renovation
	Product redesign
	Product lifecycle assessment
	Measurement and audit of Scope 1, 2 and 3 emissions[a]
	Scenario forecasting

Notes: a. GHG emissions often categorize into "scopes": Scope 1 are direct emissions produced by a business; Scope 2 are indirect emissions, from the purchase of energy and fuel; Scope 3 are all other indirect emissions that occur in a firm's value chain (MinterEllison/AICD 2021, p. 18).

Sources: Hailstone (2021); MinterEllison/AICD (2021); OECD/ASEAN (2021); SME Climate Hub (2021); Blundel and Hampton (2021); Nature Conservancy (2020).

react to events than to prepare for them (Kuruppu et al. 2013). Kato and Charoenrat (2018), for example, recently investigated the level of disaster preparation amongst Thai SMEs and found that most firms had no preparations in place to deal with an EWE; only those businesses who had already fallen victim to a natural disaster were likely to bother trying to prevent another adverse outcome. This is despite the fact that EWEs are also likely to be relatively more damaging, and more likely to threaten the viability of small firms than larger firms, who often have greater capacity to survive such challenges (Skouloudis et al. 2020). EWEs can lead to unexpected financial and physical losses and damages, and may result in stranded assets as some geographic areas become increasingly prone to disaster events.

These results are also echoed in one of the few research studies done in Southeast Asia to examine very small firms in the informal sector. Ngin, Chhom and Neef (2020) examined the repercussions of floods, droughts, storms and heatwaves on tourism-sector microbusinesses in one regional Cambodian town, and found that businesses generally adopted temporary reactive responses to the issue, rather than embark on long-term proactive measures. They also noted that there frequently are "ripple effects" from such losses, with damage to one firm often causing problems for other businesses in the same community. They concluded that these firms frequently needed not only physical and financial support, but also more information, if they were to successfully adapt to climate change.

A final, fourth emerging theme in much recent discussion on climate adaptation has been the need to advise, educate and assist firms in making the transition (OECD/ASEAN 2021; Crick et al. 2018).

One of the common findings of many researchers has been an advice and information gap. Many SMEs report that they do not have access to sufficient support services to become more climate-friendly (OECD/ASEAN 2021; Blundel and Hampton 2021; Dougherty-Choux et al. 2015). These managers recognize that they often lack the in-house skills and capabilities to reduce emissions, do not possess the needed information, and do not understand how to implement a climate change agenda, and report that they usually receive insufficient assistance from external parties (such as government bodies) to make this adjustment.

This issue builds into broader research globally which shows that SMEs can frequently suffer from information asymmetry. Many of them do not have the requisite knowledge and skills needed to best understand the climate issues facing them, accurately assess what changes might be made by their firm, and the ability to enact these (OECD/ERIA 2018). As a result, there is a growing demand for informational and advisory support to be delivered through multilateral agencies, national and local governments, and industry associations. However, the mechanics of effective information dissemination amongst SMEs are often poorly understood and ineffective (Schaper 2014).

An assistance gap is not unique to the issue of climate change adaptation or adjustment. Many other fields of small business research have also identified a shortfall in support mechanisms (see, for example, Blundel and Gray 2012; Schaper 2014). Part of this is due to the nature of SME information-seeking, which is often quite different from that of large corporations or professional researchers. Much of it is intensely personal, and based on the individual preferences and biases of the owner-manager, rather than being conducted in a dispassionate, logical manner. Small firm managers tend to be ad hoc users of data, usually only seeking answers when problems become immediate and pressing. They usually also seek information that is directly relevant, easily understandable, and complete, rather than generalized discussions of an issue. Small firms also tend to draw upon sources that they are already familiar with, and so place a large measure of reliance on their accountant, other businesspeople, industry associations, and friends and family members; government sources of information are often not used in the first instance (Kassim, Norliya and Buyong 2009).

Interestingly, government assistance is often ranked in many surveys as one of the most difficult sources for SMEs to access. In part, this is because much government information is presented in a very different manner to the way SME operators work. For example, many government agencies over-rely on web-based delivery and exclude or reduce the possibility of face-to-face support; they also often assume SMEs readers will have a working knowledge of the different branches of government; and present information in a prolix manner with many generalizations and few practical action steps (Blundel and Gray 2012; Schaper 2014).

There are still a number of gaps in the body of knowledge, especially with regards to Southeast Asia. Policymakers currently have insufficient knowledge about the following key questions:

1. How important is climate change to the managers of SMEs?
2. What climate change abatement activities, if any, are SMEs undertaking at the moment?
3. What adaptation activities are SMEs likely to undertake in the near-term future?
4. What are preferred sources of assistance and advice that SME operators need to successfully manage their reduction of carbon emissions and their adaptation to a warmer future?

THE CHALLENGES OF RESEARCHING CLIMATE CHANGE ADAPTATION AMONGST SMEs

Researching climate change adaptation is not easy in the SME sector, as small firms are perhaps the hardest of all business sectors to accurately survey or interrogate.

Some of this is due to the inherent nature of very small enterprises. As noted, SME researchers Curran and Blackburn (2001) have pointed out that small firms are hard to reach in large numbers; are less likely to capture or collect enterprise data; have little inclination to participate in external studies; are highly heterogenous (making it difficult to generalize the results found in one sector to another); and vary significantly between the self-employed, micro firms, small business, and medium enterprises.

Adaptation by SMEs to climate change is also extremely difficult to validly measure. Numerous different forms of climate adaptation exist, ranging from physical changes to technological ones. Skouloudis et al. (2020: 11) have noted that it is difficult to develop effective scalable measures that can be used over a wide range of different SMEs to accurately measure their current activities and future approaches. Different responses may also be required in different geographic zones with different localized climate issues. Adaptation will also be affected by the industry the firm operates in (a hotel will be very different to a management consultancy, a dental practice or an electrical contractor). Emissions in service sector industries are harder to identify and measure than those found in manufacturing or transport. Finally, self-employed and micro-sized businesses working from home will have a different range of adjustment options compared to larger employing enterprises operating from commercial premises (Linnenluecke and Smith 2018).

Given all of these challenges, it is perhaps not surprising that a recent critique of SME data collection and statistics by ASEAN concluded that it is usually difficult to collect accurate small firm data in the region. It recommends using a highly pragmatic, simplified approach in order to improve response rates and validity, including the use of shorter questionnaires, new technologies to reach emerging firms, and a narrowing of questions to only the most specific, relevant issues (ASEAN/OECD 2021).

METHODOLOGY

In order to answer the above four research questions, an online survey instrument was developed and applied to some 800 SME owner-operators across a wide mix of firm sizes and industries from five of the largest ASEAN economies (Indonesia, Malaysia, the Philippines, Singapore and Vietnam). In keeping with the recommendations of prior researchers noted above, it focused on the development of a very simple, quickly administered and easy-to-use generic questionnaire, which it is hoped other researchers may also use in future for other SME research into this topic.

A simple series of basic indicators was developed, deliberately designed to be as applicable as possible to a wide range of SMEs in as many different industries. This is in contrast to most other studies which have attempted to measure SME climate change activities with industry-related questions that are thus highly context-specific, applicable only to a limited number of firms, and difficult to apply across the whole spectrum of SMEs (see, for example, Herrman and Guenther 2017).

In this way it sought to bring into scope the self-employed and micro-firms that have traditionally been omitted from many studies, as well as those in low-emitting, comparatively "clean" industries which many previous studies have overlooked.

This approach, and the questions within the survey instrument itself, were refined using a Delphi technique, in which a pool of nine different professional SME researchers and academics were asked to evaluate content validity, structure, format and presentation of the tool. These researchers were drawn from a variety of institutions in Southeast Asia, Australia, New Zealand and western Europe, whose inputs resulted in a number of refinements to the questionnaire and analysis. The survey was then pre-tested on a small number of SME owner-operators.

Due to COVID-19-imposed travel constraints and the difficulty of personally interviewing respondents, an online survey tool was utilized, with respondents sourced from a panel provider. COVID-19 limitations also meant that sampling was restricted to those Southeast Asian nations with easily-accessible online respondent panels.

RESULTS

A total of 800 responses were received, representing a wide range of SMEs. In keeping with one of the principal goals of the study—making observations from across the whole SME community, rather than just a few substrata within it—the respondents represented a diverse mix of countries and industry sectors, with firms of different sizes and ages.

The respondents represented a wide cross-measure of the many different sized firms within the broader SME sector. Whilst the number of self-employed persons responding was quite low, the data set included a large number of both micro-sized and medium-sized enterprises (see Figure 1).

Responding firms were also reasonably well distributed in terms of their age (see Figure 2). There was a large proportion of recent start-ups, as well as a large number of older firms; there was an especially large number of older enterprises (i.e., those that had been trading for more than ten years).

As Figure 3 shows, there were almost equal response numbers from Malaysia, Indonesia and Vietnam. A somewhat smaller set of responses

Figure 1: Respondents by Firm Size

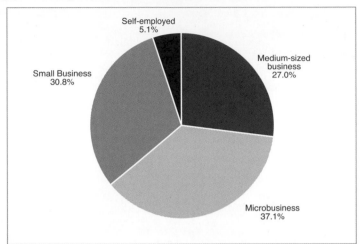

Note: Self-employed: only 1 person was employed in the business; microbusiness: 2–10 employees; small business: 11–50 employees; medium-sized business: 51–100 employees.

Figure 2: Age of Respondent Firms

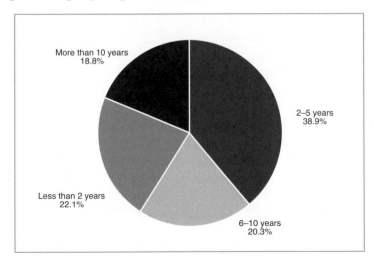

Figure 3: Distribution of Respondents by Country

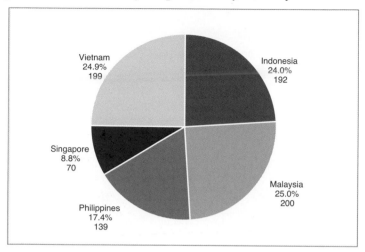

were received from the Philippines, whilst those from Singapore were fewest in number.

Respondents were drawn from a wide range of different industries, as shown in Figure 4, with the largest cohort being those in the trades sector, followed by manufacturing and services. So-called "other industries" were an especially large cohort.

Due to the lack of consistent ASEAN-wide business statistics or SME data (discussed earlier in this paper), it was not possible to compare these four descriptive characteristics against the broader small firm population. As such, it is not possible to state whether or not these respondent distributions are similar to, or vary widely from, national or regional norms.

The results indicate a number of clear patterns of behaviour amongst respondent firms.

Climate change is clearly an important issue for most firms. When asked to rate how much significance they placed on the issue, respondents gave a regionwide mean score of 6.99 out of a potential maximum of 10 (see Figure 5). There were some marked differences in these results, with (perhaps surprisingly) Filipino respondents rating the issue highest and

Figure 4: Principal Industry of Respondents

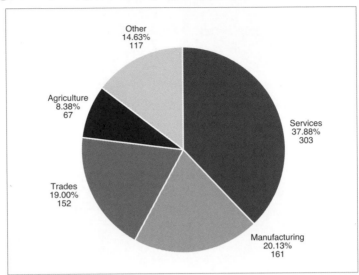

Figure 5: How Important is Climate Change to Your Business?

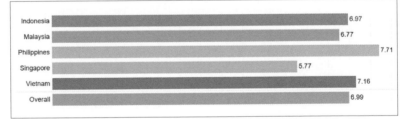

Note: Results measured on a scale of 1 (lowest) to 10 (highest).

Singaporeans reporting the lowest mean score.[4] This reflects a number of other recent studies which have also shown a marked variance in environmental concerns across the region, with the Philippines usually attaching most concern and Singapore the least (Hicks 2021).

Respondents were also asked to nominate which activities they were currently undertaking to deal with climate change issues; the results are shown in Table 6. Most firms were active in some work or another, with only a small proportion (just under 7 per cent) indicating that they were doing nothing at present.

The most common activities were the installation of low-energy lighting; recycling; reducing the use of air conditioning; and turning off of electrical devices when not in use. Notably, many of these are so-called "low hanging fruit" actions—that is, relatively simple activities that can be easily undertaken by most businesses with a minimum of financial outlay or specialist knowledge. There was also a noticeable degree of variation in responses between SMEs in different nations.

When asked what further activities businesses might be undertaking to deal with future extreme weather events (Table 7), three distinct actions were clearly favoured: reducing emissions of the business; developing a disaster or emergency plan to deal with the immediate consequences of EWE; and re-assessing the firm's insurance arrangements. However, it is notable that the level of activity varies significantly from country to country.

Respondents were also asked to identify the factors that make it difficult for them to effectively deal with climate-related issues (Table 8). Two immediate concerns rated most highly: a lack of knowledge or relevant specialist information, and insufficient funds to meet any associated expenses.

Finally, respondents were also asked two questions related to advice and assistance in dealing with climate change issues for their firm. In

---

[4] There was a statistically significant, but very weak, correlation between firm size and level of climate concern (i.e., larger firms were slightly more concerned than younger ones), with $rs = 0.1$. There was no statistically significant correlation between firm age and level of climate change concern.

Table 6: Which of the Following Activities Is Your Business Currently Doing?

	Indonesia	Malaysia	Philippines	Singapore	Vietnam	Overall
Turning off office or factory electrical devices when not in use	29.69%	41.00%	48.92%	38.57%	34.67%	37.88%
Installing low-energy lighting	31.77%	37.50%	46.76%	28.57%	39.70%	37.50%
Recycling waste materials where possible	21.88%	47.50%	52.52%	28.57%	28.64%	35.88%
Reducing air conditioning usage	26.56%	41.50%	39.57%	28.57%	31.66%	34.00%
Buying recycled/low emissions products/ materials for your business to use	25.00%	25.50%	28.06%	17.14%	25.63%	25.13%
Staff training in environmental/climate change issues	18.75%	25.50%	33.81%	12.86%	19.10%	22.63%
Using renewable energy sources for electricity	13.54%	22.50%	26.62%	12.86%	21.11%	19.88%
Product redesign to reduce energy usage or emissions	12.50%	20.50%	31.65%	22.86%	15.58%	19.50%
Building retrofits/renovation to reduce energy usage or emissions	12.50%	20.50%	18.71%	15.71%	19.60%	17.63%
Participating in an environmental certification scheme	11.98%	21.00%	30.94%	11.43%	12.56%	17.63%
Using electric or hybrid vehicles	9.90%	15.00%	13.67%	8.57%	20.10%	14.25%
Energy audits of business usage	6.25%	14.00%	19.42%	11.43%	18.09%	13.88%
Measuring the business's scope 1, 2 and 3 emissions	8.33%	18.00%	10.79%	2.86%	17.09%	12.88%
None of the above	6.25%	9.50%	5.04%	20.00%	1.51%	6.88%
Other	5.21%	5.00%	2.88%	5.71%	1.01%	3.75%

Note: Multiple responses possible.

Table 7: Which of the Following Actions are You Planning to Undertake in the Next Two Years to Deal with Extreme Weather Events?

	Indonesia	Malaysia	Philippines	Singapore	Vietnam	Total
Reduce emissions	48.44%	52.00%	52.52%	42.86%	33.67%	45.88%
Develop a disaster/emergency plan	29.69%	40.50%	61.15%	31.43%	40.70%	40.75%
Review business insurance policies	32.29%	44.00%	35.97%	27.14%	47.74%	39.25%
Relocate office(s) to a more secure location	30.73%	31.50%	38.13%	11.43%	36.68%	32.00%
None of the above	6.77%	8.50%	5.04%	21.43%	3.02%	7.25%
Other	1.56%	2.00%	1.44%	2.86%	1.01%	1.63%

Note: Multiple responses possible.

Table 8: What Obstacles Does Your Business Face in Dealing with Climate Change?

	Indonesia	Malaysia	Philippines	Singapore	Vietnam	Total
Limited access to finance	36.46%	43.50%	43.17%	28.57%	40.70%	39.75%
Limited knowledge and information about the issue	32.29%	50.00%	30.22%	40.00%	41.71%	39.38%
Limited staff skills	33.85%	39.00%	30.22%	32.86%	32.16%	34.00%
Too busy with other business issues	20.83%	32.00%	32.37%	22.86%	32.16%	28.63%
Government regulations and laws	26.56%	34.50%	33.81%	21.43%	18.59%	27.38%
Other	3.13%	4.50%	4.32%	7.14%	2.01%	3.75%

Note: Multiple responses possible.

regards to where (what sources) respondents would go for information, advice, support and/or training, government bodies were nominated as the most significant (Table 9), followed by business associations (such as a chamber of commerce or the like), friends and family, and advice on social media. Long-standing professional sources of advice (such as accountants, banks and universities) were seen as the least valuable.

There were significant variations in these patterns from one reporting country to another. Government sources were highly ranked by firms in the Philippines and Malaysia, for example, but not in Vietnam. Vietnamese respondents were far more likely than any other country to turn to a chamber of commerce, accountant or bank for advice. Personal networks, family and friends were ranked most highly in the Philippines, but lowest in Singapore.

The survey also asked respondents to indicate their preferred means of having information delivered to them (Table 10). Social media, YouTube and websites were overwhelmingly the dissemination modes of choice, whereas helplines, printed guides and seminars/workshops were seen as the least valued.

Once again, a measure of variation from one country to the next is notable. As a case in point, social media is very highly relied upon in the Philippines and Indonesia, but much less so in Vietnam or Singapore. Singaporeans express the lowest preference for face-to-face interactions, whereas it is most highly valued in neighbouring Malaysia. YouTube is seen as useful in most nations except Singapore. Seminars and workshops remain popular in the Philippines, but rate very lowly in Vietnam.

WHAT DOES THE EVIDENCE SHOW US?

Overall, these results confirm some pre-existing research on the SME sector, whilst also showing unusual results in others.

Most SME business operators/managers have a high level of concern about climate change, recording a high mean score when asked to judge its importance to their firms. This is an important original finding, as there are few previous studies which have explicitly assessed whether or not SMEs believe climate change is significant (Linnenluecke and Smith 2018).

Table 9: Which of the Following Advice Sources Would You Use?

	Indonesia	Malaysia	Philippines	Singapore	Vietnam	Total
Government agency or department	41.15%	66.00%	68.35%	52.86%	33.67%	51.25%
Chamber of commerce/industry association	35.94%	39.50%	34.53%	20.00%	41.71%	36.63%
Family or friends	30.21%	35.00%	45.32%	24.29%	36.68%	35.13%
Social media	29.69%	32.50%	43.88%	37.14%	20.10%	31.13%
Other business owners or managers	27.08%	31.00%	40.29%	22.86%	24.62%	29.38%
University or research centre	12.50%	16.50%	35.25%	14.29%	11.06%	17.25%
My bank	13.02%	16.50%	6.47%	10.00%	23.12%	15.00%
My accountant	7.81%	17.00%	6.47%	7.14%	26.63%	14.50%
My lawyer	7.81%	14.50%	6.47%	5.71%	18.59%	11.75%
Other	2.08%	4.00%	0.72%	5.71%	1.51%	2.50%

Note: Multiple responses possible.

Table 10: What is the Best Way to Deliver Advice and Information on Climate Change?

	Indonesia	Malaysia	Philippines	Singapore	Vietnam	Total
Social media	76.56%	72.50%	86.33%	51.43%	38.69%	65.63%
YouTube	55.21%	59.00%	51.80%	28.57%	61.31%	54.75%
Websites	39.58%	44.50%	33.81%	48.57%	39.20%	40.50%
Emails	28.13%	43.00%	30.94%	32.86%	44.22%	36.75%
General media (TV, radio, newspapers, magazines, etc.)	31.25%	39.50%	49.64%	25.71%	30.65%	35.88%
Face-to-face	28.65%	41.00%	30.22%	18.57%	36.18%	33.00%
Seminar and workshops	21.35%	27.50%	43.88%	15.71%	10.05%	23.50%
Printed paper pamphlets and guidebooks	8.33%	27.00%	28.06%	15.71%	18.09%	19.50%
Telephone help lines	15.63%	19.00%	10.79%	7.14%	26.13%	17.50%
Other	1.56%	2.00%	0.72%	4.29%	1.01%	1.63%

Note: Multiple responses possible.

Almost all firms are actively engaged (at least in some way) with attempts to deal with climate change and reduce emissions, typically tending to adopt the simplest and most obvious measures available to them. There is a marked preference by SMEs to adopt straightforward measures, consistent with the observations made by many other researchers that this is typical behaviour amongst smaller firms when dealing with a wide range of operational or managerial decisions. More expensive, complex, longer-term actions are far less likely to be embraced.

The research has also identified clear barriers to climate change reduction and adaptation. Most respondent businesses indicate that insufficient finance, limited knowledge, and limited inhouse staff skills and capability make the task of climate adaptation more difficult. This finding, too, echoes those of previous researchers into the topic (Blundel and Hampton 2021).

The use of business advisory and informational services shows some very mixed signals compared to previous studies. Overall, there is a very strong preference for information from government, which sits at odds with the results of many other previous studies into trusted sources of advice for SMEs. In most cases of earlier research, government has typically been one of the *least* preferred sources of information, not the most favoured. These results thus suggest that there are comparatively higher levels of trust in public officials amongst the SME community in Southeast Asia than is the case in most other parts of the world. That said, the next most-trusted options (industry associations and friends/family) are commonly cited in many SME surveys worldwide as some of the most enduringly popular advice sources. As was also noted above, there are significant variations in preferences from one country to another.

The means of delivery of potential SME assistance has also produced some different results to prior research internationally into this topic. The very heavy reliance upon online information delivery shown in this study is more pronounced than in previous other studies, but this is perhaps not surprising, since the trend over the last decade in many countries has been for SMEs to increasingly prefer more electronic information delivery. However, few other regions of the world have shown as marked a preference as this study. In part this may be a sampling bias—

respondents to this study were largely drawn from online databases—but it may also be reflective of a strong preference across Southeast Asia for online services in many aspects of commercial and private life.

AN AGENDA FOR ACTION

What are the implications of these findings, and how might they help policymakers, industry associations, and climate change advocates to work with SMEs? Five steps seem clear:

Focus on easy pickings (low hanging fruits). Emphasize the simple, straightforward actions that SMEs can easily implement within their own businesses. As the study here has shown, SMEs usually prefer making small, easy changes rather than big ones. Indeed, prior research evidence suggests that firms are typically unlikely to embrace complex, difficult or time-consuming change programmes to reduce emissions. But given the very large size of the sector, even small individual emissions reductions have the potential to generate large total impacts. A programme to replace light bulbs with more efficient, free globes, for example, may generate more emissions reductions, and be taken up by more small businesses, than more complex and costly policy solutions.

Financial support is crucial. Numerous respondents have indicated financial constraints as a major barrier to future emissions reductions and climate change/EWE adaptation. This has long been identified as a major issue for SMEs, who typically have limited financial capacity of their own to finance additional emissions-reducing outlays. There is thus clearly a continuing need for public policy support in the form of grants, discounts, soft loans or the like to assist smaller firms.

Educate to empower firms. Respondents continue to report a lack of specific, detailed knowledge about how to undertake emissions reductions and climate adaptation preparation. There is a clear role here for governments, industry bodies and NGOs to provide support, principally in the form of information and knowledge. However, such education needs to be pragmatic in nature—focused clearly on helping firms and suggesting immediate the "low hanging fruits" identified above.

Localize support. The data show some marked differences from one country to another with regards to preferred sources of advice, as well as how that assistance is delivered. It would be a mistake to adopt a "one size fits all" approach right across Southeast Asia in educating, advising, financing and supporting firms. Instead, policymakers need to work with the local preferences of SME operators.

Go online with advice and assistance. Most firms seem to have a clear comfort with accessing support, advice and information from online sources. Governments, industry bodies and advocacy groups should continue to support this, whilst also ensuring that such information remains easily accessible, uses a simple and direct language, and focuses on practical steps for immediate action. At the same time, there remains a very large proportion of firms who still turn to more traditional, intensive, face-to-face methods for their information.

CONCLUSION

Small business operators in the region *do* care about climate change. That provides a solid basis for encouraging SMEs to do more to deal with their own emissions and incorporate adaptation measures, as it is almost always easier to generate change in a community when its members recognize the significance of the problem they are confronted with and are asked to act upon. The small business sector, it seems, is well aware of the problems caused by climate change.

Most of the tools that we need to help SMEs move to a low-carbon situation, a net-zero position or even a drawdown are now well documented and available, in some way or another. The challenge is not to create new tools; it is to ensure that what governments already have is used most efficiently, and by as many small firms as possible.

Individually small but cumulatively significant, SMEs have an important role to play in turning the tide on climate change.

REFERENCES

Amran, Azlan, Say Keat Ooi, Wong Cheng Yew, and Fathyah Hashim. 2016. "Business Strategy for Climate Change: An ASEAN Perspective". *Corporate Social Responsibility and Environmental Management* 23, no. 4: 213–27.

ASEAN. 2021. "ASEAN Cooperation on Climate Change". https://environment.asean.org/asean-working-group-on-climate-change/ (accessed 6 August 2021).

ASEAN/OECD. 2021. *Strengthening Evidence-Based MSMEs Policymaking in ASEAN: Building Up More Robust, Timely, Comparable and Accessible Business Statistics.* Jakarta: ASEAN/OECD.

Asian Development Bank. 2020. *Asia Small and Medium-Sized Enterprise Monitor 2020: Vol. 1 – Country and Regional Reviews* (October). Manila: ADB.

Blundel, R., and C. Gray. 2012. *Quarterly Survey of Small Business in Britain* 28, no. 2. Milton Keynes: Open University Business School.

Blundel, Richard, and Sam Hampton. 2021. "How Can SMEs Contribute To Net Zero? An Evidence Review". *State of the Art Review*, no. 51 (July). Warwick: Enterprise Research Centre.

Carbon Trust. 2020. *SMEs and Energy Efficiency*. London: The Carbon Trust.

Crick, Florence, Shaik M.S.U. Eskander, Sam Fankhauser, and Mamadou Diop. 2018. "How Do African SMEs Respond to Climate Risks? Evidence from Kenya and Senegal". *World Development*, no. 108 (August): 157–68.

Curran, James, and Robert A. Blackburn. 2001. *Researching the Small Enterprise*. London: Sage.

Dougherty-Choux, Lisa, Pieter Terpstra, Srilata Kammila, and Pradeep Kurukulasuriya. 2015. *Adapting from the Ground Up: Enabling Small Business in Developing Countries to Adapt to Climate Change*. Washington, DC: World Resources Institute/UNDP.

Global Carbon Project. 2021. "Fossil Fuel Emissions". http://www.globalcarbonatlas.org/en/CO2-emissions (accessed 8 December 2021).

Hailstone, Jamie. 2021. "Why Small Business Need To Think About Climate Change Too". *Air Quality News*, 4 February 2021. https://airqualitynews.com/2021/02/04/why-small-businesses-need-to-think-about-climate-change-too/ (accessed 26 August 2021).

Herrman, Jana, and Edeltraud Guenther. 2017. "Exploring a Scale of Organizational Barriers for Enterprises' Climate Change Adaptation Strategies". *Journal of Cleaner Production*, no. 160: 38–49.

Hicks, Robin. 2021. "How Much Do Southeast Asians Care about Environmental and Social Issues?". *Ecobusiness*, 12 October 2021. https://www.eco-business.com/news/how-much-do-southeast-asians-care-about-environmental-and-social-issues/ (accessed 8 December 2021).

Intergovernmental Panel on Climate Change. 2014. *Climate Change 2014: Mitigation of Climate Change.* Cambridge: Cambridge University Press.

———. 2021. "Summary for Policymakers". In *Climate Change 2021: The Physical Science Basis. Contribution of Working Group I to the Sixth Assessment Report of the Intergovernmental Panel on Climate Change*, edited by V. Masson-Delmotte, P. Zhai, A. Pirani, S.L. Connors, C. Péan, S. Berger, N. Caud, Y. Chen, L. Goldfarb, M.I. Gomis, M. Huang, K. Leitzell, E. Lonnoy, J.B.R. Matthews, T.K. Maycock, T. Waterfield, O. Yelekçi, R. Yu, and B. Zhou. Cambridge University Press.

Kassim, N.A., Norliya, Ahmad M., and S.Z. Buyong. 2009. *Business Information Needs and Managing Information Among Malaysian Bumiputera Entrepreneurs.* Shah Alam: Institute of Research, Development and Commercialization, Universiti Teknologi MARA.

Kato, Mio, and Teerawat Charoenrat. 2018. "Business Continuity Management of Small and Medium Sized Enterprises: Evidence from Thailand". *International Journal of Disaster Risk Reduction*, no. 27: 577–87.

Kuruppu, Natasha, Janina Murta, Pierre Mukheibir, Joanne Chong, and Tim Brennan. 2013. *Understanding the Adaptive Capacity of Australian Small-to-Medium Enterprises to Climate Change and Variability.* Gold Coast: National Climate Change Adaptation Research Facility.

Lamb, William F., and Thomas Wiedmann. 2021. "A Review of Trends and Drivers of Greenhouse Gas Emissions by Sector from 1990 to 2018". *Environmental Research Letters* 16, no. 7: 3005.

Linnenluecke, Martina, and Tom Smith. 2018. "Adaptation of MSMEs to Climate Change: A Review of the Existing Literature". In *Private-Sector Action in Adaptation: Perspectives on the Role of Micro, Small and Medium Size Enterprises,* edited by Caroline Schaer and Natasha Kuruppu, pp. 19–27. Copenhagen: UNEP DTU Partnership.

MinterEllison/AICD. 2021. *Climate Risk Governance Guide: An Introductory Resource for Directors,* (August). Sydney: Australian Institute of Company Directors.

Nature Conservancy. 2020. *Carbon Sustainability Playbook: A Roadmap for Small and Medium Enterprises Ready for Climate Action.* Minneapolis: Nature Conservancy for Minnesota, North Dakota and South Dakota.

Ngin, Chanrith, Chanchhaya Chhom, and Andreas Neef. 2020. "Climate Change Impacts and Disaster Resilience Among Micro Businesses in the Tourism and Hospitality Sector: The Case of Kratie, Cambodia". *Environmental Research,* no. 186 (July): 109557 ff.

OECD/ASEAN. 2021. *Facilitating the Green Transition for ASEAN SMEs: A Toolkit for Policymakers,* Paris: OECD. https://asean.org/storage/Facilitating-Green-Transition-for-ASEAN-SMEs.pdf

OECD/Economic Research Institute for ASEAN and East Asia. 2018. "Environmental Policies and SMEs". In *SME Policy Index: ASEAN 2018: Boosting Competitiveness and Inclusive Growth.* Paris: OECD Publishing; Jakarta: Economic Research Institute for ASEAN and East Asia.

Schaefer, Anja, Sarah Williams, and Richard Blundel. 2020. "Individual Values and SME Environmental Engagement". *Business and Society* 59, no. 4: 642–75.

Schaer, Caroline, and Natasha Kuruppu, eds. 2018. *Private-Sector Action in Adaptation: Perspectives on the Role of Micro, Small and Medium Size Enterprises.* Copenhagen: UNEP DTU Partnership.

Schaper, Michael T. 2014. "Is Anybody Listening? Improving Government Information and Communication to Small Business". In *Meeting the Globalisation Challenge: Smart and Innovative SMEs in a Globally Competitive Environment*, edited by B. Kotey, T. Mazzarol, D. Clark, D. Foley, and T. McKeown, pp. 134–51. Melbourne: Tilde.

———. 2019. "Motivations and Barriers to Going Green Amongst Australian Businesses: Identifying the On and Off Switches in Small, Medium and Large Firms". In *Sustainable Entrepreneurship: Discovering, Creating and Seizing Opportunities for Blended Value Generation*, edited by A. Lindgreen, F. Maon, C. Vallaster, S. Yousofzai, and B. Palacios Florencio, pp. 255–65. Abingdon: Routledge.

———. 2020. "The Missing (Small) Businesses of Southeast Asia". *ISEAS Perspectives,* no. 2020/79, 22 July 2020.

Seah, Sharon, Melinda Martinus, and Qiu Jiahui. 2021. *Southeast Asia Climate Outlook: 2021 Survey Report*. Singapore: ISEAS – Yusof Ishak Institute.

Skouloudis, Antonis, Thomas Tsalis, Ioannis Nikolaou, Konstantinos Evangelinos, and Walter Leal Filho. 2020. "Small and Medium-Sized Enterprises, Organizational Resilience Capacity and Flash Floods: Insights From A Literature Review". *Sustainability* 12, no. 18: 7437ff.

SME Climate Hub. 2021. "Tools and Resources: Real Business Support Starts Here". https://smeclimatehub.org/tools/ (accessed 10 September 2021).

Storbeck, Olaf. 2018. "Smaller Is Best in German Effort to Hit Green Targets: Mittelstand". *Financial Times*, 5 December 2018., p. 2.

Swiss Re Institute. 2021. "The Economics of Climate Change: No Action Not an Option". April, Zurich. swiss-re-institute-expertise-publication-economics-of-climate-change.pdf (swissre.com) (accessed 18 August 2021).

UNFCCC/UNESCAP. 2021. "Building SMEs Capacity on Climate Action: Experiences from South-East Asia". Draft Concept Note, July 2021. 25.06 -Draft CN and Agenda - Side event on CB Needs. pdf (unfccc.int) (accessed 9 August 2021).

Williams, Sarah, and Anja Schaefer. 2012. "Small and Medium-Sized Enterprises and Sustainability: Managers' Values and Engagement with Environmental and Climate Change Issues". *Business Strategy and the Environment* 22, no. 3: 173–86.

Zurich Insurance. 2016. *Potential Effect on Business of Small and Medium Enterprises (SMEs) Due to Climate Change in 2016.* November. Zurich: Zurich Insurance Company.